GAUGE INFORMATION

With smaller size hook
and Main Color,
16 sts = 4" (10 cm)

Gauge Swatch: 4"w x 2"h
(10 cm x 5 cm)

With smaller size hook and Main Color, ch 18.

Row 1: Dc in fourth ch from hook **(3 skipped chs count as first dc)** and in each ch across: 16 dc.

Rows 2-4: Ch 3 **(counts as first dc)**, turn; dc in next dc and in each dc across.

Finish off.

CHANGING COLORS

Drop yarn, to join new yarn with slip st, insert hook in first st, with new yarn, YO and draw through st and loop on hook ***(Fig. A)***.

Fig. A

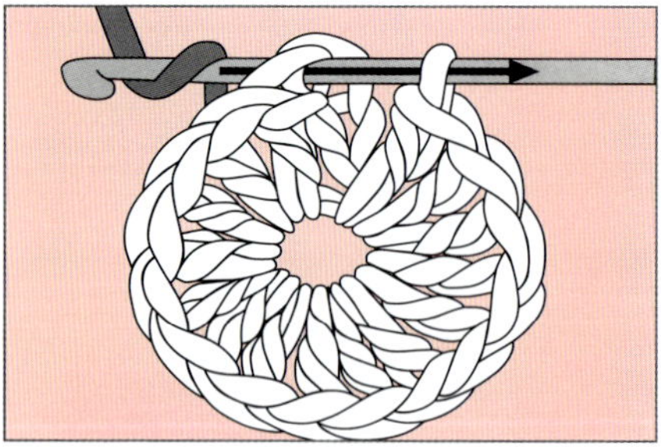

INSTRUCTIONS

BODY

With smaller size hook and Contrasting Color, ch 60{68-72}; being careful **not** to twist ch, join with slip st to form a ring.

Rnd 1 (Right side)**:** Ch 2 **(counts as first hdc, now and throughout)**, hdc in next ch and in each ch around; drop Contrasting Color to back, with Main Color, join with slip st to first hdc ***(Fig. A)***, do **not** cut Contrasting Color: 60{68-72} hdc.

Note: Loop a short piece of yarn around any stitch to mark Rnd 1 as **right** side.

Rnd 2: Ch 3 **(counts as first dc, now and throughout)**, dc in same st as joining and in next 4{4-5} hdc, ★ 2 dc in next hdc, dc in next 4{6-5} hdc; repeat from ★ around; drop Main Color to back, with Contrasting Color, join with slip st to first dc: 72{78-84} dc.

Best-Dressed Baby

Offered in a delightful range of solids and ombres, Bernat® Softee® Baby™ is a premium light weight acrylic yarn that has been a customer favorite for baby projects for decades. Bernat® Pipsqueak™ is a bulky weight polyester yarn that creates a soft fuzzy look; it works up quickly and comes in a fun range of colors. Both yarns can be machine washed and dried for easy care.

About Spinrite:

Established in 1952, Spinrite LP is North America's largest craft yarn producer. Its well-known brands include Patons, Bernat, Caron, and Lily Sugar 'n Cream. For more about Spinrite, visit Yarnspirations.com, a one-stop resource for everything that you need to create knit and crochet projects to suit any mood, budget, or occasion.

LEISURE ARTS, INC.
Maumelle, Arkansas

Lacy Poncho

EASY

SHOPPING LIST

Yarn

Bernat® Softee® Baby™ LIGHT 3
(Light Weight)
[5 ounces, 362 yards
(140 grams, 331 meters)
per skein]:

- ☐ Main Color, #02001 Pink - 1 skein
- ☐ Contrasting Color, #30010 Little Mouse - 45 yards (41 meters)

Bernat® Pipsqueak™ BULKY 5
(Bulky Weight)
[3.5 ounces, 120 yards
(100 grams, 109 meters)
per skein]:

- ☐ Edging, #59005 Whitey White - 40 yards (36.5 meters)

Crochet Hooks

- ☐ Size G (4 mm) **or** size needed for gauge
- ☐ Size I (5.5 mm) for Edging only

SIZE INFORMATION

Finished Measurements:

Small - 14" neck x $6^1/_2$" length (35.5 cm x 16.5 cm)

Medium - 16" neck x $7^1/_2$" length (40.5 cm x 19 cm)

Large - 17" neck x $8^1/_2$" length (43 cm x 21.5 cm)

Size Note: We have printed the instructions for the sizes in different colors to make it easier for you to find:

- · Small in Blue
- · Medium in Pink
- · Large in Green

Instructions in Black apply to all sizes.

Rnd 3: Ch 1, sc in same st as joining, ch 1 **loosely**, skip next dc, ★ sc in next dc, ch 1 **loosely**, skip next dc; repeat from ★ around; join with slip st to first sc: 36{39-42} sc and 36{39-42} ch-1 sps.

Rnd 4: Ch 1, turn; sc in same st as joining, ch 1 **loosely**, (sc in next sc, ch 1 **loosely**) around; drop Contrasting Color to front, with Main Color, join with slip st to first sc.

Rnd 5: Ch 1, turn; sc in same st as joining, ★ working in **front** of previous 2 rnds, dc in skipped dc in rnd **below** ***(Fig. B)***, sc in next sc; repeat from ★ around; join with slip st to first sc: 72{78-84} sts.

Fig. B

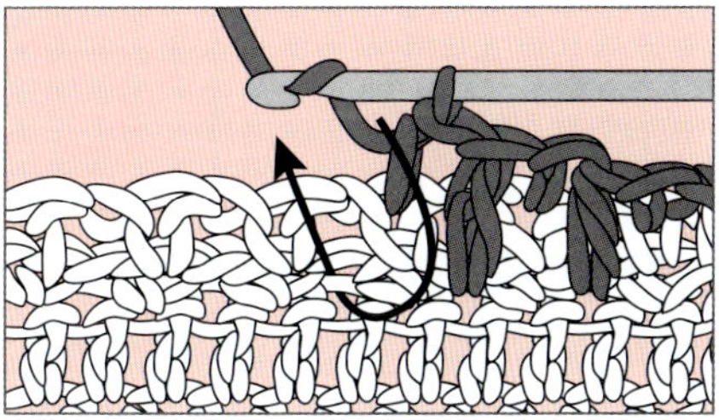

Rnd 6: Ch 1, turn; sc in same st as joining and in next 2{4-2} sts, 2 sc in next st, ★ sc in next 5{5-6} sts, 2 sc in next st; repeat from ★ around to last 2{6-3} sts, sc in last 2{6-3} sts; drop Main Color to front, with Contrasting Color, join with slip st to first sc: 84{90-96} sc.

Rnd 7: Ch 1, turn; sc in same st as joining, ch 1 **loosely**, skip next sc, ★ sc in next sc, ch 1 **loosely**, skip next sc; repeat from ★ around; join with slip st to first sc: 42{45-48} sc and 42{45-48} ch-1 sps.

Rnd 8: Ch 1, turn; sc in same st as joining, ch 1 **loosely**, (sc in next sc, ch 1 **loosely**) around; cut Contrasting Color, with Main Color, join with slip st to first sc.

Rnd 9: Ch 1, turn; sc in same st as joining, working in **front** of previous 2 rnds, dc in skipped sc in rnd **below**, ★ sc in next sc, working in **front** of previous 2 rnds, dc in skipped sc in rnd **below**; repeat from ★ around; join with slip st to first sc: 84{90-96} sts.

Rnd 10: Ch 1, turn; sc in each st around; join with slip st to first sc.

Rnd 11: Ch 5, turn; dc in same st as joining, skip next 2 sc, ★ dc in next sc, (ch 2, dc) twice in same st, skip next 2 sc; repeat from ★ around; dc in same st as first dc, ch 1, sc in third ch of beginning ch-5 to form last ch-2 sp: 56{60-64} ch-2 sps.

Rnd 12: Ch 1, turn; sc in last ch-2 sp made, (ch 3, sc in next ch-2 sp) around; ch 1, hdc in first sc to form last ch-3 sp: 56{60-64} ch-3 sps.

Rnd 13: Ch 5, turn; dc in last ch-3 sp made, skip next ch-3 sp, ★ dc in next ch-3 sp, (ch 2, dc) twice in same sp, skip next ch-3 sp; repeat from ★ around; dc in same sp as first dc, ch 1, sc in third ch of beginning ch-5 to form last ch-2 sp: 56{60-64} ch-2 sps.

Repeat Rnds 12 and 13 until Body measures approximately 5{6-7}"/ 12.5{15-18} cm from beginning ch, ending by working Rnd 13: 56{60-64} ch-2 sps.

Next Rnd: Ch 1, turn; sc in last ch-2 sp made, ch 3, (sc in next ch-2 sp, ch 3) around; join with slip st to first sc, finish off: 56{60-64} ch-3 sps.

Last Rnd: With **right** side facing, join Contrasting Color with slip st in first ch-3 sp; ch 2, hdc in same sp, 2 hdc in next ch-3 sp and in each ch-3 sp around; join with slip st to top of beginning ch-2, finish off: 112{120-128} sts.

Edging: With **right** side facing and using larger size hook, join Bulky Weight Yarn with sc in same st as joining *(Fig. 3, page 47)*; skip next hdc, (sc in next hdc, skip next hdc) around; join with slip st to first sc, finish off.

NECK EDGING

With **right** side facing, using larger size hook, and working in free loops of beginning ch *(Fig. 2b, page 46)*, join Bulky Weight Yarn with slip st in first ch; ch 1, sc in same st, skip next ch, (sc in next ch, skip next ch) around; join with slip st to first sc, finish off.

Design by Cathy Hardy.

Muff

EASY

Shown on page 3.

Finished Size: 6" wide x 9" circumference (15 cm x 23 cm)

SHOPPING LIST

Yarn

Bernat® Pipsqueak™ BULKY 5
(Bulky Weight)
[3.5 ounces, 120 yards
(100 grams, 109 meters)
per skein]:
- ☐ #59005 Whitey White - 1 skein

Crochet Hook

- ☐ Size I (5.5 mm) **or** size needed for gauge

GAUGE INFORMATION

9 dc = 4" (10 cm)

Gauge Swatch: 4" (10 cm) wide
Ch 11.

Row 1: Dc in fourth ch from hook **(3 skipped chs count as first dc)** and in each ch across: 9 dc.

Rows 2-4: Ch 3 **(counts as first dc)**, turn; dc in next dc and in each dc across.

Finish off.

INSTRUCTIONS

Ch 20; being careful not to twist ch, join with slip st to form a ring.

Rnd 1: Ch 3 **(counts as first dc)**, dc in next st and in each st around; join with slip st to first dc: 20 dc.

Repeat Rnd 1 for pattern until Muff measures approximately 6" (15 cm) from beginning ch; finish off.

Bubble Suit

INTERMEDIATE

SHOPPING LIST

Yarn

Bernat® Softee® Baby™ LIGHT 3
(Light Weight)
[5 ounces, 362 yards
(140 grams, 331 meters)
per skein]:

- ☐ Main Color, #30185 Soft Lilac - 2 skeins
- ☐ Contrasting Color, #02000 White - 1 skein

Crochet Hooks

- ☐ Size D (3.25 mm) **and**
- ☐ Size G (4 mm)

or sizes needed for gauge

Additional Supplies

- ☐ Tapestry needle
- ☐ Sewing needle and thread
- ☐ 1/2" (12 mm) Buttons - 4
- ☐ Elastic cord - 14" (35.5 cm)

SIZE INFORMATION

Finished Chest Measurement:
3 Months - 18" (45.5 cm)
6 Months - 19" (48.5 cm)

Size Note: We have printed the instructions for the sizes in different colors to make it easier for you to find:

- 3 Months in Blue
- 6 Months in Pink

Instructions in Black apply to both sizes.

GAUGE INFORMATION

With larger size hook,
9 dc and 5 rows = 2 1/4" (5.75 cm)

Gauge Swatch: 2 1/4" (5.75 cm) square

With larger size hook, ch 11.

Row 1: Dc in fourth ch from hook **(3 skipped chs count as first dc)** and in each ch across: 9 dc.

Rows 2-5: Ch 3 **(counts as first dc)**, turn; dc in next dc and in each dc across.

Finish off.

STITCH GUIDE

FRONT POST SINGLE CROCHET

(abbreviated FPsc)

Insert hook from **front** to **back** around post of stitch indicated *(Fig. A)*, YO and pull up a loop, YO and draw through both loops on hook.

Fig. A

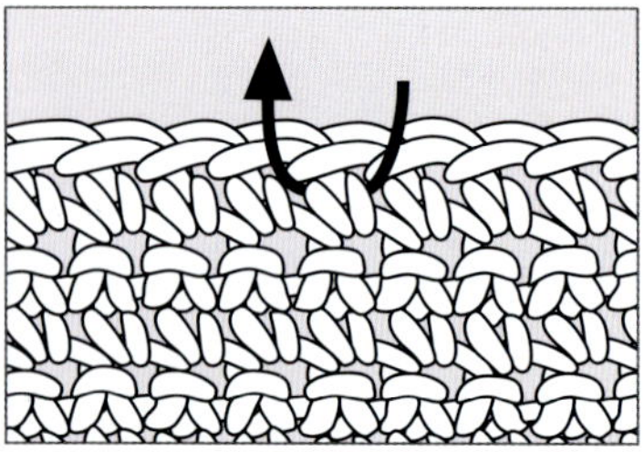

INSTRUCTIONS

Use larger size hook throughout, unless otherwise specified.

FRONT YOKE

With Main Color, ch 25{27}.

Row 1 (Right side)**:** Sc in second ch from hook and in each ch across: 24{26} sc.

Note: Loop a short piece of yarn around any stitch to mark Row 1 as **right** side.

Rows 2-4: Ch 1, turn; sc in each sc across.

Row 5: Ch 3 **(counts as first dc, now and throughout)**, turn; working in Back Loops Only *(Fig. 1, page 46)*, dc in same st and in each sc across to last sc, 2 dc in last sc: 26{28} dc.

Rows 6-8: Ch 3, turn; working in both loops, dc in same st and in each dc across to last dc, 2 dc in last dc: 32{34} dc.

Row 9: Ch 3, turn; 2 dc in same st, dc in next dc and in each dc across to last dc, 3 dc in last dc: 36{38} dc.

Size 3 Months Only: Finish off.

Size 6 Months Only - Row 10: Ch 3, turn; dc in next dc and in each dc across; finish off.

LEFT SHOULDER

Row 1: With **right** side of Front Yoke facing and working in free loops of beginning ch *(Fig. 2b, page 46)*, join Main Color with sc in first ch *(Fig. 3, page 47)*; sc in next 5 chs, leave remaining chs unworked: 6 sc.

Rows 2 thru 7{9}: Ch 1, turn; sc in each sc across.

Finish off.

Row 8{10}: Ch 6{7}; with **wrong** side of Left Shoulder facing, sc in each sc across; do **not** finish off: 6 sc and 6{7} chs.

LEFT BACK YOKE

Row 1: Ch 1, turn; sc in each sc and in each ch across: 12{13} sc.

Rows 2-4: Ch 1, turn; sc in each sc across.

Row 5: Ch 3, turn; dc in Back Loop Only of same st and each sc across: 13{14} dc.

Row 6: Ch 3, turn; working in both loops, dc in next dc and in each dc across to last dc, 2 dc in last dc: 14{15} dc.

Row 7: Ch 3, turn; dc in same st and in each dc across: 15{16} dc.

Row 8: Ch 3, turn; dc in next dc and in each dc across to last dc, 2 dc in last dc: 16{17} dc.

Row 9: Ch 3, turn; 2 dc in same st, dc in next dc and in each dc across: 18{19} dc.

Size 3 Months Only: Finish off.

Size 6 Months Only - Row 10: Ch 3, turn; dc in next dc and in each dc across; finish off.

RIGHT SHOULDER

Row 1: With **right** side of Front Yoke facing and working in free loops of beginning ch, skip 12{14} chs from Left Shoulder and join Main Color with sc in next ch; sc in next 5 chs: 6 sc.

Rows 2 thru 8{10}: Ch 1, turn; sc in each sc across; do **not** finish off.

RIGHT BACK YOKE

Row 1: Ch 7{8}, turn; sc in second ch from hook and in each ch and each sc across: 12{13} sc.

Rows 2-4: Ch 1, turn; sc in each sc across.

Row 5: Ch 3, turn; working in Back Loops Only, dc in next sc and in each sc across to last sc, 2 dc in last sc: 13{14} dc.

Row 6: Ch 3, turn; dc in both loops of same st and each dc across: 14{15} dc.

Row 7: Ch 3, turn; dc in next dc and in each dc across to last dc, 2 dc in last dc: 15{16} dc.

Row 8: Ch 3, turn; dc in same st and in each dc across: 16{17} dc.

Row 9: Ch 3, turn; dc in next dc and in each dc across to last dc, 3 dc in last dc: 18{19} dc.

Size 3 Months Only: Finish off; with **right** side facing, join Main Color with slip st in first dc on Right Back Yoke.

Size 6 Months Only - Row 10: Ch 3, turn; dc in next dc and in each dc across; do **not** finish off.

BODY

Row 1: With **right** side facing, ch 3, dc in same st and in each dc across; with **right** side of Front Yoke facing, dc in each dc across; with **right** side of Left Back Yoke facing, dc in each dc across to last dc, 2 dc in last dc: 74{78} dc.

Row 2: Ch 3, turn; (dc, ch 1, dc) in next dc, ★ skip next dc, (dc, ch 1, dc) in next dc; repeat from ★ across to last 2 dc, skip next dc, dc in last dc: 36{38} ch-1 sps.

Rows 3 thru 8{10}: Ch 3, turn; (2 dc, ch 1, 2 dc) in each ch-1 sp across, dc in last dc.

Begin working in rounds.

Rnd 1: Ch 3, turn; (2 dc, ch 1, 2 dc) in each ch-1 sp across, dc in last dc, ch 3 (placket); join with slip st to first dc: 36{38} ch-1 sps and one ch-3.

Rnd 2: Do **not** turn; slip st in next 2 dc and in next ch-1 sp, ch 3, (dc, ch 1, 2 dc) in same sp, (2 dc, ch 1, 2 dc) in next ch-1 sp and in each ch-1 sp around to ch-3, (2 dc, ch 1, 2 dc) in center ch of ch-3; join with slip st to first dc: 37{39} ch-1 sps.

Rnd 3: Slip st in next dc and in next ch-1 sp, ch 3, (dc, ch 1, 2 dc) in same sp, (2 dc, ch 1, 2 dc) in next ch-1 sp and in each ch-1 sp around to last ch-1 sp, 2 dc in last ch-1 sp, (ch 1, 2 dc in same sp) twice; join with slip st to first dc: 38{40} ch-1 sps.

Rnds 4-8: Slip st in next dc and in next ch-1 sp, ch 3, (dc, ch 1, 2 dc) in same sp, (2 dc, ch 1, 2 dc) in next ch-1 sp and in each ch-1 sp around; join with slip st to first dc, do **not** finish off.

FIRST LEG

Rnd 1: Slip st in next dc and in next ch-1 sp, ch 3, (dc, ch 1, 2 dc) in same sp, (2 dc, ch 1, 2 dc) in next 18{19} ch-1 sps, leave remaining sps unworked; join with slip st to first dc: 19{20} ch-1 sps.

Rnds 2 thru 11{13}: Slip st in next dc and in next ch-1 sp, ch 3, (dc, ch 1, 2 dc) in same sp, (2 dc, ch 1, 2 dc) in next ch-1 sp and in each ch-1 sp around; join with slip st to first dc.

Rnd 12{14}: Slip st in next dc and in next ch-1 sp, ch 1, sc in same sp and in each ch-1 sp around; join with slip st to first sc: 19{20} sc.

Size 3 Months ONLY - Rnd 13: Ch 3, dc in same st as joining, ★ dc in next 2 sc, 2 dc in next sc; repeat from ★ around; join with slip st to first dc: 26 dc.

Size 6 Months ONLY - Rnd 15: Ch 3, dc in same st as joining and in next sc, ★ 2 dc in next sc, dc in next 2 sc; repeat from ★ around; join with slip st to first dc: 27 dc.

Both Sizes

Rnd 14{16}: Ch 1, sc in same st and in each dc around; join with slip st to first sc, finish off.

Rnd 15{17}: With **right** side facing and using smaller size hook, join Contrasting Color with sc in any sc; ch 3, (sc in next sc, ch 3) around; join with slip st to first sc, finish off.

SECOND LEG

Rnd 1: With **right** side facing, join Main Color with slip st in first skipped ch-1 sp on Rnd 8 of Body; ch 3, (dc, ch 1, 2 dc) in same sp, (2 dc, ch 1, 2 dc) in next 18{19} ch-1 sps; join with slip st to first dc: 19{20} ch-1 sps.

Complete same as First Leg.

Sew opening closed.

FINISHING

RIGHT PLACKET

Row 1: With **right** side facing and working in end of rows on Right Back Yoke and Body, join Main Color with sc in Row 1; work 31{35} sc evenly spaced across: 32{36} sc.

Row 2 (Buttonhole row)**:** Ch 1, turn; sc in first 6{10} sc, ch 2, skip next sc (buttonhole), ★ sc in next 7 sc, ch 2, skip next sc (buttonhole); repeat from ★ 2 times **more**, sc in last sc; finish off.

LEFT PLACKET

Row 1: With **right** side facing and working in end of rows on Body and Left Back Yoke, join Main Color with sc in last row of Body; work 31{35} sc evenly spaced across: 32{36} sc.

Row 2: Ch 1, turn; sc in each sc across; do **not** finish off.

PLACKET & NECK TRIM

Ch 1, turn; sc in each sc across to last sc, 2 sc in last sc; sc in end of each row on Plackets and Shoulders and in free loop of each ch on Yokes; 2 sc in first sc on Right Placket, sc in each sc and in each ch-2 sp across; finish off.

ARMHOLE TRIM

With **right** side facing, join Main Color with sc at underarm; work 39{41} sc evenly spaced around; join with slip st to first sc, finish off.

Repeat on second Armhole.

YOKE RUFFLE

With **right** side of neck opening facing you, using smaller size hook, and working in free loops on Row 4 of Right Back Yoke *(Fig. 2a, page 46)*, join Contrasting Color with sc in first sc; ch 3, (sc in next sc, ch 3) across; working in Front Loops Only of sc on Armhole Trim *(Fig. 1, page 46)*, (sc in next sc, ch 3) across to free loops of sc on Row 4 of Front Yoke; working in free loops on Row 4 of Front Yoke, (sc in next sc, ch 3) across; working in Front Loops Only of sc on Armhole Trim, (sc in next sc, ch 3) across to free loops of sc on Row 4 of Left Back Yoke; working in free loops on Row 4 of Left Back Yoke, sc in next sc, (ch 3, sc in next sc) across; finish off.

Beginning at the inside of each Leg, weave an elastic cord through the bottom of the dc on Rnd 13{15}; tie the ends together and hide the ends.

FLOWER (Make 3)

With Contrasting Color, smaller size hook, and leaving a long end for sewing, ch 4; join with slip st to form a ring.

Rnd 1 (Right side)**:** Ch 1, (sc in ring, ch 3) 5 times; join with slip st to first sc: 5 ch-3 sps.

Note: Mark Rnd 1 as **right** side.

Rnd 2: Ch 1, (sc, 5 dc, sc) in each ch-3 sp around; join with slip st to first sc: 5 petals.

Rnd 3: Ch 1, working in **front** of petals and around sc on Rnd 1, work FPsc around first sc *(Fig. A, page 10)*, ch 2, (FPsc around next sc, ch 2) around; join with slip st to first FPsc: 5 ch-2 sps.

Rnd 4: Ch 1, (sc, 3 dc, sc) in each ch-2 sp around; join with slip st to first sc, finish off.

Using photo as a guide for placement, sew three Roses to Front Yoke.

Sew buttons to Button Band opposite buttonholes.

Design by Sandra Abbate.

Flowers Blanket

EASY

Finished Size: 33" x 35" (84 cm x 89 cm)

SHOPPING LIST

Yarn

Bernat® Softee® Baby™ LIGHT 3
(Light Weight)
[5 ounces, 362 yards
(140 grams, 331 meters)
per skein]:

- ☐ Green, #02004 Mint - 4 skeins

Bernat® Pipsqueak™ BULKY 5
(Bulky Weight)
[3.5 ounces, 120 yards
(100 grams, 109 meters)
per skein]:

- ☐ Pink, #59421 Tickle Me Pink - 2 skeins

Crochet Hooks

- ☐ Size G (4 mm) **and**
- ☐ Size I (5.5 mm)
  or sizes needed for gauge

Additional Supplies

- ☐ Tapestry needle and yarn needle

GAUGE INFORMATION

One Motif = $3^1/_2$" (9 cm) (straight edge to straight edge)
Gauge Swatch: 2" (5 cm) diameter
Work same as Motif Rnd 1.

STITCH GUIDE

ADJUSTABLE LOOP

Wind yarn around two fingers to form a ring *(Fig. A)*. Slide yarn off fingers and grasp the strands at the top of the ring *(Fig. B)*. Insert hook from front to back into the ring, pull up a loop, YO and draw through loop on hook to lock ring *(Fig. C)*. Working around both strands, follow instructions to work sts in the ring, then pull yarn tail to close *(Fig. D)*.

Fig. A

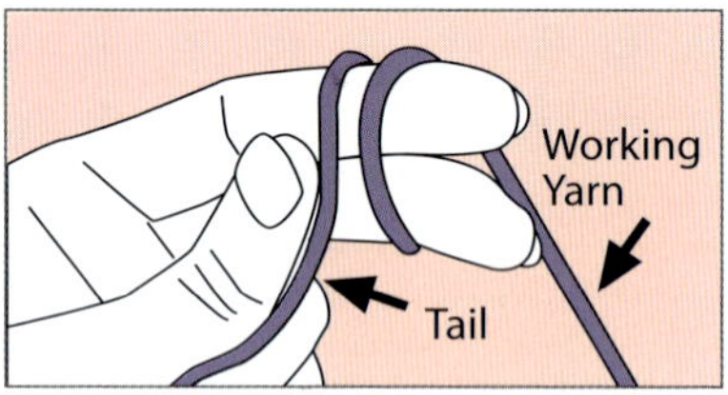

Fig. B

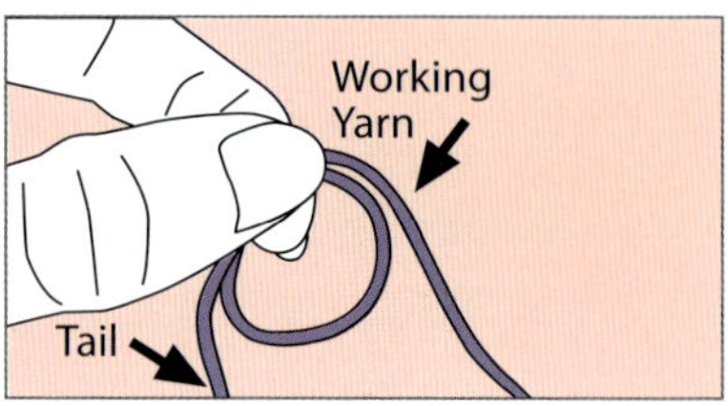

Fig. C

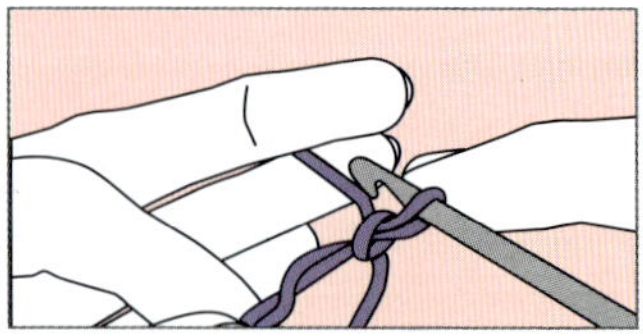

Fig. D

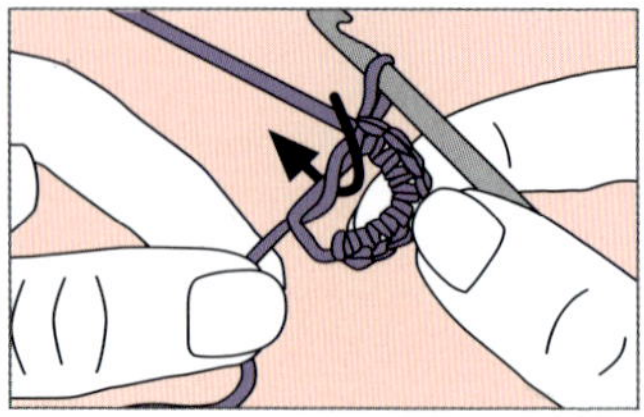

BEGINNING CLUSTER
(uses one sp)

Ch 2, ★ YO, insert hook in same sp, YO and pull up a loop, YO and draw through 2 loops on hook; repeat from ★ once **more**, YO and draw through all 3 loops on hook.

CLUSTER (uses one sp)

★ YO, insert hook in sp indicated, YO and pull up a loop, YO and draw through 2 loops on hook; repeat from ★ 2 times **more**, YO and draw through all 4 loops on hook.

INSTRUCTIONS

MOTIF (Make 94)

Rnd 1 (Right side)**:** With larger size hook and Pink, make an adjustable loop to form a ring; (sc in ring, ch 3) 6 times; join with slip st to first sc, finish off: 6 sc and 6 ch-3 sps.

Note: Loop a short piece of yarn around any stitch to mark Rnd 1 as **right** side.

Rnd 2: With **right** side facing and smaller size hook, join Green with slip st in any ch-3 sp; work (Beginning Cluster, ch 3, Cluster) in same sp, ch 1, ★ work (Cluster, ch 3, Cluster) in next ch-3 sp, ch 1; repeat from ★ around; join with slip st to top of Beginning Cluster: 12 Clusters and 12 sps.

Rnd 3: Slip st in first ch-3 sp, ch 3 **(counts as first dc, now and throughout)**, (2 dc, ch 2, 3 dc) in same sp, ch 1, 3 dc in next ch-1 sp, ch 1, ★ (3 dc, ch 2, 3 dc) in next ch-3 sp, ch 1, 3 dc in next ch-1 sp, ch 1; repeat from ★ around; join with slip st to first dc, finish off: 54 dc and 18 sps.

HALF MOTIF (Make 10)

Row 1 (Right side)**:** With larger size hook and Pink, make an adjustable loop; sc in ring, (ch 3, sc in ring) 4 times; do **not** join, finish off: 5 sc and 4 ch-3 sps.

Note: Mark Row 1 as **right** side.

Row 2: With **wrong** side facing and smaller size hook, join Green with dc in first ch-3 sp *(Fig. 4, page 47)*; ch 1, work Cluster in same sp, ch 1, ★ work (Cluster, ch 3, Cluster) in next ch-3 sp, ch 1; repeat from ★ once **more**, work (Cluster, ch 1, dc) in last ch-3 sp: 6 Clusters, 2 dc, and 7 sps.

Row 3: Ch 4 **(counts as first dc plus ch 1)**, turn; (3 dc in next ch-1 sp, ch 1) twice, (3 dc, ch 2, 3 dc) in next ch-3 sp, ch 1, 3 dc in next ch-1 sp, ch 1, (3 dc, ch 2, 3 dc) in next ch-3 sp, ch 1, (3 dc in next ch-1 sp, ch 1) twice, dc in last dc; finish off: 29 dc and 10 sps.

ASSEMBLY

Using Placement Diagram as a guide and Green, hold **wrong** sides together and whipstitch Motifs together working through **inside** loops only, *(Fig. 5a, page 47)*, beginning in second ch of first corner ch-2 and ending in first ch of next corner ch-2, forming 6 horizontal strips of 9 Motifs each.

Whipstitch 8 Motifs and 2 Half Motifs together forming 5 horizontal strips, then whipstitch all strips together in same manner.

PLACEMENT DIAGRAM

TRIM

With **right** side facing, using smaller size hook, and working across long edge of Blanket, join Green with sc in first dc after corner ch-2 sp *(Fig. 3, page 47)*; sc in next 2 dc, (skip next ch-1 sp, sc in next 3 dc) twice, ★ skip next joining, working across end of rows on Half Motif, 2 sc in each of next 3 rows, 2 sc in adjustable ring, 2 sc in each of next 3 rows, skip next joining, sc in next 3 dc, (skip next ch-1 sp, sc in next 3 dc) twice; repeat from ★ 4 times **more**; finish off: 124 sc.

Work Trim on second long edge.

EDGING

With **right** side facing and using larger size hook, join Pink with sc in first sc on either long edge; † (ch 1, skip next 2 sc, sc in next sc) across long edge; ch 1, sc in next sp, (ch 1, skip next 3 dc, sc in next sp) 6 times, ★ skip next joining and next 3 dc, sc in next sp, (ch 1, skip next 3 dc, sc in next sp) 5 times; repeat from ★ 7 times **more**, ch 1, sc in next corner sp, ch 1 †, sc in next sc on long edge, repeat from † to † once; join with slip st to first sc, finish off.

Design by Sandra Abbate.

Ribbed Hat

EASY

Shown on page 23.

SHOPPING LIST

Yarn

Bernat® Softee® Baby™
(Light Weight)
[4.25 ounces, 310 yards
(120 grams, 283 meters)
per skein]:

- ☐ #31201 Prince Pebbles Ombre - 1 skein

Crochet Hook

- ☐ Size E (3.5 mm)
  or size needed for gauge

Additional Supplies

- ☐ Tapestry needle

SIZE INFORMATION

Finished Circumference:

Small - 14" (35.5 cm)
Medium - 15" (38 cm)
Large - 16" (40.5 cm)

Size Note: We have printed the instructions for the sizes in different colors to make it easier for you to find:

- Small in Blue
- Medium in Pink
- Large in Green

Instructions in Black apply to all sizes.

GAUGE INFORMATION

In ribbing, 5 sc and 6 rows = 1" (2.5 cm),
In pattern, (sc, ch 1) 4 times = 1" (2.5 cm)

Gauge Swatch: 2" (5 cm) square

Ch 11.

Row 1: Sc in second ch from hook and in each ch across: 10 sc.

Rows 2-12: Ch 1, turn; sc in Back Loop Only of each sc across *(Fig. 1, page 46)*.

Finish off.

INSTRUCTIONS

Ch 60{66-72}.

Row 1 (Right side)**:** Sc in second ch from hook and in next 6{8-10} chs (ribbing), ★ ch 1, skip next ch, sc in next ch; repeat from ★ across: 33{37-41} sc and 26{28-30} chs.

Note: Loop a short piece of yarn around any stitch to mark Row 1 as **right** side.

Work in Back Loops Only throughout ***(Fig. 1, page 46)***.

Row 2: Ch 1, turn; sc in first sc, ch 1, ★ skip next ch, sc in next sc, ch 1; repeat from ★ across to last 8{10-12} sts, skip next ch, sc in last 7{9-11} sc.

Row 3: Ch 1, turn; sc in first 7{9-11} sc, ★ ch 1, skip next ch, sc in next sc; repeat from ★ across.

Repeat Rows 2 and 3 until Hat measures approximately 14{15-16}"/35.5{38-40.5} cm from beginning ch at widest end, ending by working Row 2.

Finish off leaving a long end for sewing.

Fold Hat with **wrong** side together. Using long end, matching sts, and working in free loops of beginning ch ***(Fig. 2b, page 46)*** **and** through inside loops of sts on last row, whipstitch edge together ***(Fig. 5a, page 47)***. With **wrong** side facing, weave yarn end through one loop at the end of every other row at top; gather tightly and secure end.

Make a pom-pom ***(Figs. 6a-c, page 48)*** and sew to top of Hat.

Turn ribbing up to form a cuff.

Design by Valesha Marshell Kirksey.

Heart Blanket

EASY

Finished Size: 35" x 45½" (89 cm x 115.5 cm)

SHOPPING LIST

Yarn

Bernat® Softee® Baby™ (LIGHT 3)
(Light Weight)
[5 ounces, 362 yards
(140 grams, 331 meters)
per skein**]**:

- ☐ #02001 Pink - 3 skeins

Crochet Hook

- ☐ Size F (3.75 mm)
  or size needed for gauge

Additional Supplies

- ☐ Tapestry needle

GAUGE INFORMATION

In pattern,
 16 sts and 8 rows = 4" (10 cm)
 One Panel = 10¼" (26 cm) wide

Gauge Swatch: 4" (10 cm) square

Ch 18.

Row 1: Dc in fourth ch from hook **(3 skipped chs count as first dc)** and in each ch across: 16 dc.

Rows 2-8: Ch 3 **(counts as first dc)**, turn; dc in next dc and in each dc across.

Finish off.

INSTRUCTIONS

PANEL (Make 3)

Ch 43, place a marker in third ch from hook for st placement.

Row 1 (Right side)**:** Dc in fourth ch from hook **(3 skipped chs count as first dc)** and in next 2 chs, ch 1, ★ skip next ch, dc in next 3 chs, ch 1; repeat from ★ across to last 5 chs, skip next ch, dc in last 4 chs: 32 dc and 9 ch-1 sps.

Note: Loop a short piece of yarn around any stitch to mark Row 1 as **right** side and bottom edge.

Row 2: Ch 3 **(counts as first dc, now and throughout)**, turn; dc in next dc, ch 1, ★ skip next dc, dc in next dc and in next ch-1 sp, dc in next dc, ch 1; repeat from ★ across to last 3 dc, skip next dc, dc in last 2 dc: 31 dc and 10 ch-1 sps.

Row 3: Ch 3, turn; dc in next dc and in next ch-1 sp, ★ dc in next dc, ch 1, skip next dc, dc in next dc and in next ch-1 sp; repeat from ★ across to last 2 dc, dc in last 2 dc: 32 dc and 9 ch-1 sps.

Row 4: Ch 3, turn; dc in next dc, ch 1, ★ skip next dc, (dc in next dc, ch 1) twice; repeat from ★ across to last 3 dc, skip next dc, dc in last 2 dc: 22 dc and 19 ch-1 sps.

Row 5: Ch 3, turn; dc in next dc and in next ch-1 sp, dc in next dc, (ch 1, dc in next dc) across to last ch-1 sp, dc in last ch-1 sp and in last 2 dc: 24 dc and 17 ch-1 sps.

Row 6: Ch 3, turn; dc in next dc, ch 1, skip next dc, (dc in next dc, ch 1) across to last 3 dc, skip next dc, dc in last 2 dc: 22 dc and 19 ch-1 sps.

Row 7: Ch 3, turn; dc in next dc and in next ch-1 sp, ★ (dc in next dc, ch 1) 8 times, dc in next dc and in next ch-1 sp; repeat from ★ once **more**, dc in last 2 dc: 25 dc and 16 ch-1 sps.

Row 8: Ch 3, turn; dc in next dc, ch 1, skip next dc, (dc in next dc, ch 1) 7 times, dc in next dc and in next ch-1 sp, dc in next 3 dc and in next ch-1 sp, (dc in next dc, ch 1) 8 times, skip next dc, dc in last 2 dc.

Row 9: Ch 3, turn; dc in next dc and in next ch-1 sp, (dc in next dc, ch 1) 6 times, dc in next dc and in next ch-1 sp, dc in next 3 dc, ch 1, skip next dc, dc in next 3 dc and in next ch-1 sp, (dc in next dc, ch 1) 6 times, dc in next dc and in next ch-1 sp, dc in last 2 dc: 28 dc and 13 ch-1 sps.

Row 10: Ch 3, turn; dc in next dc, ch 1, skip next dc, (dc in next dc, ch 1) 5 times, dc in next dc and in next ch-1 sp, dc in next 3 dc, ch 1, skip next dc, (dc in next dc, ch 1) twice, skip next dc, dc in next 3 dc and in next ch-1 sp, (dc in next dc, ch 1) 6 times, skip next dc, dc in last 2 dc: 26 dc and 15 ch-1 sps.

Row 11: Ch 3, turn; dc in next dc and in next ch-1 sp, (dc in next dc, ch 1) 4 times, dc in next dc and in next ch-1 sp, dc in next 3 dc, ch 1, skip next dc, (dc in next dc, ch 1) 4 times, skip next dc, dc in next 3 dc and in next ch-1 sp, (dc in next dc, ch 1) 4 times, dc in next dc and in next ch-1 sp, dc in last 2 dc: 28 dc and 13 ch-1 sps.

Row 12: Ch 3, turn; dc in next dc, ch 1, skip next dc, (dc in next dc, ch 1) 3 times, dc in next dc and in next ch-1 sp, dc in next 3 dc, ch 1, skip next dc, (dc in next dc, ch 1) 6 times, skip next dc, dc in next 3 dc and in next ch-1 sp, (dc in next dc, ch 1) 4 times, skip next dc, dc in last 2 dc: 26 dc and 15 ch-1 sps.

Row 13: Ch 3, turn; dc in next dc and in next ch-1 sp, (dc in next dc, ch 1) twice, dc in next dc and in next ch-1 sp, dc in next 3 dc, ch 1, skip next dc, (dc in next dc, ch 1) 3 times, dc in next dc and in next ch-1 sp, (dc in next dc, ch 1) 4 times, skip next dc, dc in next 3 dc and in next ch-1 sp, (dc in next dc, ch 1) twice, dc in next dc and in next ch-1 sp, dc in last 2 dc: 29 dc and 12 ch-1 sps.

Row 14: Ch 3, turn; dc in next dc, ch 1, skip next dc, (dc in next dc, ch 1) twice, dc in next 5 dc, ch 1, (dc in next dc, ch 1) 3 times, dc in next 3 dc, ch 1, (dc in next dc, ch 1) 3 times, dc in next 5 dc, ch 1, (dc in next dc, ch 1) twice, skip next dc, dc in last 2 dc: 27 dc and 14 ch-1 sps.

Row 15: Ch 3, turn; dc in next dc and in next ch-1 sp, (dc in next dc, ch 1) twice, dc in next 5 dc, ch 1, (dc in next dc, ch 1) twice, dc in next dc and in next ch-1 sp, dc in next 3 dc and in next ch-1 sp, (dc in next dc, ch 1) 3 times, dc in next 5 dc, ch 1, dc in next dc, ch 1, dc in next dc and in next ch-1 sp, dc in last 2 dc: 31 dc and 10 ch-1 sps.

Row 16: Ch 3, turn; dc in next dc, ch 1, skip next dc, (dc in next dc, ch 1) 3 times, skip next dc, ★ dc in next 3 dc and in next ch-1 sp, (dc in next dc and in next ch-1 sp) twice, dc in next 3 dc, ch 1, skip next dc; repeat from ★ once **more**, (dc in next dc, ch 1) 3 times, skip next dc, dc in last 2 dc: 32 dc and 9 ch-1 sps.

Row 17: Ch 3, turn; dc in next dc and in next ch-1 sp, (dc in next dc, ch 1) 4 times, skip next dc, dc in next 7 dc, ch 1, skip next dc, (dc in next dc, ch 1) twice, skip next dc, dc in next 7 dc, ch 1, skip next dc, (dc in next dc, ch 1) 3 times, dc in next dc and in next ch-1 sp, dc in last 2 dc: 30 dc and 11 ch-1 sps.

Row 18: Ch 3, turn; dc in next dc, ch 1, skip next dc, (dc in next dc, ch 1) 5 times, skip next dc, (dc in next dc, ch 1, skip next dc) twice, (dc in next dc, ch 1) 4 times, skip next dc, (dc in next dc, ch 1, skip next dc) twice, (dc in next dc, ch 1) 5 times, skip next dc, dc in last 2 dc: 22 dc and 19 ch-1 sps.

Row 19: Ch 3, turn; dc in next dc and in next ch-1 sp, dc in next dc, (ch 1, dc in next dc) across to last ch-1 sp, dc in last ch-1 sp and in last 2 dc: 24 dc and 17 ch-1 sps.

Row 20: Ch 3, turn; dc in next dc, ch 1, skip next dc, (dc in next dc, ch 1) across to last 3 dc, skip next dc, dc in last 2 dc: 22 dc and 19 ch-1 sps.

Row 21: Ch 3, turn; dc in next dc and in next ch-1 sp, ★ dc in next dc, ch 1, dc in next dc and in next ch-1 sp; repeat from ★ across to last 2 dc, dc in last 2 dc: 32 dc and 9 ch-1 sps.

Rows 22-83: Repeat Rows 2-21, 3 times; then repeat Rows 2 and 3 once **more**; do **not** finish off.

BORDER

With **right** side facing and working in end of rows, (slip st, ch 3, dc) in Row 83, 2 dc in next row and in each row across; working in free loops of beginning ch *(Fig. 2b, page 46)*, (2 dc, ch 2, 2 dc) in first ch, dc in each ch across to marked ch, (2 dc, ch 2, 2 dc) in marked ch; working in end of rows, 2 dc in each row across; (2 dc, ch 2, 2 dc) in first dc on Row 83, dc in each dc and in each ch across to last dc, (2 dc, ch 2, 2 dc) in last dc; join with slip st to first dc, finish off: 426 dc and 4 ch-2 sps.

ASSEMBLY

Place two Panels with **wrong** sides of long edge together and bottom edges at the same end. Working through **inside** loops, whipstitch edges together *(Fig. 5a, page 47)*, beginning in second ch of first corner and ending in first ch of next corner.

EDGING

Rnd 1: With **right** side of short edge facing, join yarn with slip st in first corner ch-2 sp; ch 5 **(counts as first dc plus ch 2)**, 2 dc in same corner sp, † ch 1, (skip next dc, dc in next 3 dc, ch 1) 10 times, skip next dc, dc in next 2 dc and in next ch, ch 1, skip next joining and next ch, dc in next 3 dc, ch 1, (skip next dc, dc in next 3 dc, ch 1) 10 times, skip next ch and next joining, dc in next ch and in next 2 dc, ch 1, skip next dc, (dc in next 3 dc, ch 1, skip next dc) 10 times, (2 dc, ch 2, 2 dc) in next corner ch-2 sp †, (ch 1, skip next dc, dc in next 3 dc) across to within 2 dc of next corner ch-2 sp, ch 1, skip next 2 dc, (2 dc, ch 2, 2 dc) in corner ch-2 sp, repeat from † to † once, ch 1, skip next 2 dc, (dc in next 3 dc, ch 1, skip next dc) across, dc in same corner sp as joining; join with slip st to first dc: 466 dc and 4 ch-2 sps.

Rnds 2 and 3: (Slip st, ch 5, 2 dc) in next corner sp, ★ † ch 1, skip next dc, (dc in next dc and in next ch-1 sp, dc in next dc, ch 1, skip next dc) across to next corner ch-2 sp †, (2 dc, ch 2, 2 dc) in corner sp; repeat from ★ 2 times **more**, then repeat from † to † once, dc in same corner sp as first dc; join with slip st to first dc.

Finish off.

Design by Mary Ann Sipes.

Booties

EASY

Size: 0-3 Months

SHOPPING LIST

Yarn

Bernat® Softee® Baby™

(Light Weight)

[5 ounces, 362 yards

(140 grams, 331 meters)

per skein**]**:

- ☐ #02001 Pink - 65 yards (59.5 meters)

Crochet Hook

- ☐ Size E (3.5 mm) **or** size needed for gauge

Additional Supplies

- ☐ Tapestry needle
- ☐ $\frac{1}{4}$" (7 mm) wide Ribbon - 32" (81.5 cm) length

GAUGE INFORMATION

In pattern, 7 dc = 1$\frac{1}{2}$" (3.75 cm)

Gauge Swatch: 3$\frac{3}{4}$" (9.5 cm) long

Work same as Sole.

STITCH GUIDE

DOUBLE CROCHET 2 TOGETHER

(abbreviated dc2tog) (uses 2 dc)

★ YO, insert hook in **next** dc, YO and pull up a loop, YO and draw through 2 loops on hook; repeat from ★ once **more**, YO and draw through all 3 loops on hook **(counts as one dc)**.

INSTRUCTIONS
SOLE

Ch 13.

Rnd 1 (Right side)**:** 3 Sc in second ch from hook, sc in next 10 chs, 5 sc in last ch; working in free loops of beginning ch *(Fig. 2b, page 46)*, sc in next 10 chs, 2 sc in next ch; join with slip st to Back Loop Only of first sc *(Fig. 1, page 46)*: 30 sc.

Note: Loop a short piece of yarn around any stitch to mark Rnd 1 as **right** side.

Rnd 2: Ch 3 **(counts as first dc, now and throughout unless otherwise indicated)**, working in Back Loops Only, 2 dc in next sc, dc in next 3 sc, hdc in next 4 sc, dc in next 4 sc, 2 dc in each of next 2 sc, dc in next sc, 2 dc in each of next 2 sc, dc in next 4 sc, hdc in next 4 sc, dc in next 3 sc, 2 dc in next sc; join with slip st to first dc, do **not** finish off: 36 sts.

SIDES

Rnd 1: Ch 3, dc in Back Loop Only of next st and each st around; join with slip st to first dc.

Rnd 2: Ch 3, dc in both loops of next dc and each dc around; join with slip st to first dc.

Rnd 3: Ch 1, sc in same st as joining and in next 11 dc, dc2tog, (dc in next dc, dc2tog) 3 times, sc in last 13 dc; join with slip st to first sc: 32 sts.

Rnd 4: Ch 1, sc in same st as joining and in next 11 sc, dc2tog 4 times, sc in last 12 sc; join with slip st to first sc: 28 sts.

CUFF

Rnd 1 (Eyelet rnd)**:** Ch 3 **(counts as first hdc plus ch 1)**, skip next st, (hdc in next st, ch 1, skip next st) 4 times, (dc in next st, ch 1, skip next st) 5 times, (hdc in next st, ch 1, skip next st) 4 times; join with slip st to first hdc: 14 ch-1 sps.

Rnd 2: Ch 1, 2 sc in each ch-1 sp around; join with slip st to first sc: 28 sc.

Rnd 3: Ch 4 **(counts as first dc plus ch 1, now and throughout)**, ★ skip next sc, dc in next 3 sc, ch 1; repeat from ★ around to last 3 sc, skip next sc, dc in last 2 sc; join with slip st to first dc: 21 dc and 7 ch-1 sps.

Rnd 4: Ch 3, dc in next ch-1 sp and in next dc, ch 1, skip next dc, ★ dc in next dc and in next ch-1 sp, dc in next dc, ch 1, skip next dc; repeat from ★ around; join with slip st to first dc.

Rnd 5: Ch 4, skip next dc, dc in next dc and in next ch-1 sp, ★ dc in next dc, ch 1, skip next dc, dc in next dc and in next ch-1 sp; repeat from ★ around; join with slip st to first dc, finish off.

Beginning at center front, weave a 16" (40.5 cm) length of ribbon through Eyelet rnd.

Design by Mary Ann Sipes.

Ear-Flap Hat

EASY

Shown on page 35.

Size: 3-6 Months

SHOPPING LIST

Yarn

Bernat® Softee® Baby™ (LIGHT 3)
(Light Weight)
[5 ounces, 362 yards
(140 grams, 331 meters)
per skein**]**:
- ☐ Main Color, #30300 Baby Denim Marl - 1 skein

Bernat® Pipsqueak™ (BULKY 5)
(Bulky Weight)
[3.5 ounces, 120 yards
(100 grams, 109 meters)
per skein**]**:
- ☐ Edging, #59128 Baby Blue - 35 yards (32 meters)

Yarn Note: The Edging can be worked with Main Color **or** with a Bulky Weight Yarn.

Crochet Hooks

- ☐ Size F (3.75 mm) **or** size needed for gauge
- ☐ Size I (5.5 mm) for Bulky Weight Yarn only

Additional Supplies

- ☐ Tapestry and yarn needle

GAUGE INFORMATION

With smaller size hook and Main Color,
16 sc and 16 rows = 3½" (9 cm)
Gauge Swatch: 2¼" (5.75 cm) diameter
Work same as Crown, page 34, through Rnd 5.

STITCH GUIDE

SINGLE CROCHET 2 TOGETHER *(abbreviated sc2tog)* (uses 2 sts)
Pull up a loop in each of next 2 sts, YO and draw through all 3 loops on hook **(counts as one sc)**.

INSTRUCTIONS

CROWN

With smaller size hook, Main Color, and beginning at center, ch 3; join with slip st to form a ring.

Rnd 1: Ch 1, 6 sc in ring; join with slip st to first sc.

Rnd 2 (Right side)**:** Ch 1, turn; 2 sc in each sc around; join with slip st to first sc: 12 sc.

Note: Loop a short piece of yarn around any stitch to mark Rnd 2 as **right** side.

Rnd 3: Ch 1, turn; sc in first sc, 2 sc in next sc, (sc in next sc, 2 sc in next sc) around; join with slip st to first sc: 18 sc.

Rnd 4: Ch 1, turn; sc in first 2 sc, 2 sc in next sc, (sc in next 2 sc, 2 sc in next sc) around; join with slip st to first sc: 24 sc.

Rnd 5: Ch 1, turn; sc in first 3 sc, 2 sc in next sc, (sc in next 3 sc, 2 sc in next sc) around; join with slip st to first sc: 30 sc.

Rnd 6: Ch 1, turn; sc in first 4 sc, 2 sc in next sc, (sc in next 4 sc, 2 sc in next sc) around; join with slip st to first sc: 36 sc.

Rnd 7: Ch 1, turn; sc in first 5 sc, 2 sc in next sc, (sc in next 5 sc, 2 sc in next sc) around; join with slip st to first sc: 42 sc.

Rnd 8: Ch 1, turn; sc in first 6 sc, 2 sc in next sc, (sc in next 6 sc, 2 sc in next sc) around; join with slip st to first sc: 48 sc.

Rnd 9: Ch 1, turn; sc in first 7 sc, 2 sc in next sc, (sc in next 7 sc, 2 sc in next sc) around; join with slip st to first sc: 54 sc.

Rnd 10: Ch 1, turn; sc in first 8 sc, 2 sc in next sc, (sc in next 8 sc, 2 sc in next sc) around; join with slip st to first sc: 60 sc.

Rnd 11: Ch 1, turn; sc in first 9 sc, 2 sc in next sc, (sc in next 9 sc, 2 sc in next sc) around; join with slip st to first sc: 66 sc.

Rnds 12-18: Ch 1, turn; sc in each sc around; join with slip st to first sc.

Rnd 19: Ch 1, do **not** turn; sc in Back Loop Only of each sc around *(Fig. 1, page 46)*; join with slip st to both loops of first sc.

Rnds 20-22: Ch 1, turn; sc in both loops of each sc around; join with slip st to first sc.

Finish off.

LEFT EAR FLAP

Row 1: With **wrong** side facing and using smaller size hook, skip first sc on Rnd 22 and place a marker in next sc for Edging placement, skip next 6 sc and join Main Color with sc in next sc *(Fig. 3, page 47)*; sc in next 9 sc: 10 sc.

Row 2: Ch 1, turn; sc in each sc across.

Row 3 (Decrease row)**:** Ch 1, turn; beginning in first sc, sc2tog, sc in each sc across to last 2 sc, sc2tog: 8 sc.

Rows 4-8: Repeat Rows 2 and 3 twice, then repeat Row 2 once **more**: 4 sc.

Row 9: Ch 1, turn; sc in first 2 sc, sc2tog: 3 sc.

Row 10: Ch 1, turn; sc in each sc across.

Row 11: Ch 1, turn; skip first sc, sc2tog; finish off.

RIGHT EAR FLAP

Row 1: With **wrong** side facing and using smaller size hook, skip next 29 sc on Rnd 22 and join Main Color with sc in next sc; sc in next 9 sc: 10 sc.

Rows 2-11: Repeat Rows 2-11 of Left Ear Flap.

EDGING

Option #1 is worked with a Bulky Weight Yarn and Option #2 is worked with Main Color. Choose desired Edging.

OPTION #1

With **wrong** side facing and using larger size hook, join Bulky Weight Yarn with sc in marked sc on Rnd 22, remove marker; sc evenly spaced around entire edge including Ear Flaps; join with slip st to first sc, finish off.

OPTION #2

With **wrong** side facing and using smaller size hook, join Main Color with sc in marked sc on Rnd 22, remove marker; dc in same sc, [skip next sc, (sc, dc) in next sc] 3 times, † working in end of rows on Ear Flap, (sc, dc) in first row, [skip next row, (sc, dc) in next row] 4 times, skip next row, (sc, dc) in turning ch of last row, (sc, dc) in next st, [skip next row, (sc, dc) in next row] 5 times †; working on Rnd 22 of Crown, [skip next sc, (sc, dc) in next sc] 14 times, skip next sc, repeat from † to † once; working on Rnd 22 of Crown, [skip next sc, (sc, dc) in next sc] 4 times; join with slip st to first sc, finish off: 94 sts.

FIRST TIE

Cut a strand of Main Color 3 yards (2.75 meters) long.

Insert smaller size hook in st on **wrong** side of bottom of Ear Flap; fold strand in half and draw fold through st. Holding both strands of yarn together, ch 38; finish off leaving a long end to finish and attach pom-pom.

SECOND TIE

Cut a piece of Main Color 4 yards (3.5 meters) long.

Insert smaller size hook in st on **wrong** side of bottom of Ear Flap; fold strand in half and draw fold through st. Holding both strands of yarn together, ch 48; finish off leaving a long end to finish and attach pom-pom.

With Main Color, make two pom-poms attaching each to a Tie using the long ends on the Tie *(Figs. 6a-c, page 48)*.

Design by Carol Holding.

Bonnet

EASY

Size: 3-6 Months

SHOPPING LIST

Yarn

Bernat® Softee® Baby™ (LIGHT 3)
(Light Weight)
[5 ounces, 362 yards
(140 grams, 331 meters)
per skein]:

- ☐ Main Color, #02003 Lemon - 1 skein

Bernat® Pipsqueak™ (BULKY 5)
(Bulky Weight)
[3.5 ounces, 120 yards
(100 grams, 109 meters)
per skein]:

- ☐ Edging, #59306 Baby Baby Print - 20 yards (18.5 meters)

Yarn Note: The Edging can be worked with Main Color **or** with a Bulky Weight Yarn.

Crochet Hooks

- ☐ Size F (3.75 mm) **or** size needed for gauge
- ☐ Size I (5.5 mm) for Bulky Weight Yarn only

Additional Supplies

- ☐ Tapestry and yarn needle

GAUGE INFORMATION

With smaller size hook and Main Color, in pattern,
16 sts and 16 rows = $3^1/_2$" (9 cm)

Gauge Swatch: $3^1/_2$" (9 cm) wide
Work same as Body through Row 2.

STITCH GUIDE

SINGLE CROCHET 2 TOGETHER
(abbreviated sc2tog)
(uses 2 sts or rows)

Pull up a loop in each of next 2 sts or rows, YO and draw through all 3 loops on hook **(counts as one sc)**.

INSTRUCTIONS

BODY

With smaller size hook, Main Color, and beginning at bottom, ch 17.

Row 1: Sc in second ch from hook and in each ch across: 16 sc.

Row 2 (Right side)**:** Ch 1, turn; (sc, dc) in first sc, ★ skip next sc, (sc, dc) in next sc; repeat from ★ across to last 3 sc, skip next sc, sc in last 2 sc: 16 sts.

Note: Loop a short piece of yarn around any stitch to mark Row 2 as **right** side.

Row 3: Ch 1, turn; 2 sc in first sc, sc in each st across to last sc, 2 sc in last sc: 18 sc.

Row 4: Ch 1, turn; sc in first sc, (sc, dc) in next sc, ★ skip next sc, (sc, dc) in next sc; repeat from ★ across to last 2 sc, skip next sc, sc in last sc: 18 sts.

Row 5: Ch 1, turn; 2 sc in first sc, sc in each st across to last sc, 2 sc in last sc: 20 sc.

Row 6: Ch 1, turn; (sc, dc) in first sc, ★ skip next sc, (sc, dc) in next sc; repeat from ★ across to last 3 sc, skip next sc, sc in last 2 sc: 20 sts.

Row 7: Ch 1, turn; sc in each st across: 20 sc.

Rows 8-46: Repeat Rows 6 and 7, 19 times; then repeat Row 6 once **more**.

Row 47: Ch 1, turn; beginning in first sc, sc2tog, sc in each st across to last 2 sts, sc2tog: 18 sc.

Row 48: Ch 1, turn; sc in first sc, (sc, dc) in next sc, ★ skip next sc, (sc, dc) in next sc; repeat from ★ across to last 2 sc, skip next sc, sc in last sc: 18 sts.

Row 49: Ch 1, turn; beginning in first sc, sc2tog, sc in each st across to last 2 sts, sc2tog: 16 sc.

Rows 50 and 51: Repeat Rows 6 and 7.

Finish off.

BACK EDGING

With **wrong** side facing, using smaller size hook, and working in end of rows, join Main Color with slip st in first row; sc in next 21 rows, sc2tog, pull up a loop in next row, skip next row, pull up a loop in next row, YO and draw through all 3 loops on hook, sc2tog, sc in next 21 rows, slip st in last row; finish off leaving a long end for sewing: 47 sts.

Fold Body in half with **wrong** side together and matching short ends. Working through **both** loops, whipstitch back seam along Back Edging *(Fig. 5b, page 47)*.

FRONT & NECK EDGING

Option #1 is worked using Main Color for Rnd 1 and a Bulky Weight Yarn for Rnd 2. Option #2 is worked in Main Color only. Choose desired Edging.

OPTION #1

Rnd 1: With **right** side facing, using smaller size hook, and working in end of rows, join Main Color with sc in first row; sc in each row across; work 37 sc evenly spaced across bottom edge of Body; join with slip st to first sc, finish off: 88 sc.

Rnd 2: With **right** side facing and using larger size hook, join Bulky Weight Yarn with sc in first sc; skip next sc, (sc in next sc, skip next sc) around; join with slip st to first sc, finish off.

OPTION #2

Front Edging

Row 1: With **right** side facing, using smaller size hook, and working in end of rows, join Main Color with sc in first row; sc in each row across: 51 sc.

Row 2: Ch 1, turn; sc in each sc across.

Row 3: Ch 1, turn; (sc, dc) in first sc, ★ skip next sc, (sc, dc) in next sc; repeat from ★ across to last 2 sc, skip next sc, sc in last sc; do **not** finish off: 51 sts.

Neck Edging

Row 1: Work 36 sc evenly spaced across bottom edge of Body including Front Edgings.

Row 2: Ch 1, turn; sc in each sc across; finish off.

FIRST TIE

Cut a strand of Main Color 3 yards (2.75 meters) long.
Insert smaller size hook in corner on **wrong** side of Neck Edging; fold strand in half and draw fold through st. Holding both strands of yarn together, ch 38; finish off leaving a long end to finish and attach pom-pom.

SECOND TIE

Cut a piece of Main Color 4 yards (3.5 meters) long.
Insert smaller size hook in corner on **wrong** side of Neck Edging; fold strand in half and draw fold through st. Holding both strands of yarn together, ch 48; finish off leaving a long end to finish and attach pom-pom.

With Main Color, make two pom-poms attaching each to a Tie using the long ends *(Figs. 6a-c, page 48)*.

Design by Carol Holding.

Hand Mitts

EASY

Size: 5" circumference at top edge x 3" long (12.5 cm x 7.5 cm)

SHOPPING LIST

Yarn

Bernat® Softee® Baby™ (LIGHT 3)
(Light Weight)
[4.25 ounces, 310 yards
(120 grams, 283 meters)
per skein]:

- ☐ #31413 Tiny Tulips Ombre - 1 skein

Crochet Hook

- ☐ Size E (3.5 mm) **or** size needed for gauge

Additional Supplies

- ☐ Tapestry needle

GAUGE INFORMATION

In pattern, 21 sts = 3" (7.5 cm)
Gauge Swatch: 3" (7.5 cm) wide
Work same as Mitt for 6 rows.

INSTRUCTIONS

Leaving a long end for sewing, ch 22.

Row 1 (Right side)**:** Sc in second ch from hook and in next 4 chs, ★ ch 1, skip next ch, sc in next ch; repeat from ★ across: 13 sc and 8 ch-1 sps.

Note: Loop a short piece of yarn around second to last sc made to mark Row 1 as **right** side and top edge.

Work in Back Loops Only throughout ***(Fig. 1, page 46)***.

Row 2: Ch 1, turn; sc in first sc, ch 1, (skip next ch, sc in next sc, ch 1) 7 times, skip next ch, sc in last 5 sc.

Row 3: Ch 1, turn; sc in first 5 sc, (ch 1, skip next ch, sc in next sc) across.

Repeat Rows 2 and 3 for pattern until Mitt measures approximately 5" (12.5 cm) from beginning ch at top edge, ending by working Row 2.

Finish off leaving a long end for sewing.

Fold Mitt with **wrong** side together. Using long ends, matching sts and working in free loops of beginning ch *(Fig. 2b, page 46)* **and** through inside loops of sts on last row, whipstitch 5 sts at top edge together *(Fig. 5a, page 47)*, and 11 sts at bottom edge together, leaving 5 sts free for thumb opening.

GENERAL INSTRUCTIONS

ABBREVIATIONS

ch	chain(s)
cm	centimeters
dc	double crochet(s)
dc2tog	double crochet 2 together
FPsc	Front Post single crochet(s)
hdc	half double crochet(s)
mm	millimeters
Rnd(s)	Round(s)
sc	single crochet(s)
sc2tog	single crochet 2 together
sp(s)	space(s)
st(s)	stitch(es)
YO	yarn over

CROCHET TERMINOLOGY		
UNITED STATES		INTERNATIONAL
slip stitch (slip st)	=	single crochet (sc)
single crochet (sc)	=	double crochet (dc)
half double crochet (hdc)	=	half treble crochet (htr)
double crochet (dc)	=	treble crochet (tr)
treble crochet (tr)	=	double treble crochet (dtr)
double treble crochet (dtr)	=	triple treble crochet (ttr)
triple treble crochet (tr tr)	=	quadruple treble crochet (qtr)
skip	=	miss

SYMBOLS & TERMS

★ — work instructions following ★ as many **more** times as indicated in addition to the first time.

( ) or **[ ]** — work enclosed instructions **as many** times as specified by the number immediately following **or** work all enclosed instructions in the stitch or space indicated **or** contains explanatory remarks.

† to † — work all instructions from first † to second † **as many** times as specified.

colon (:) — the number(s) given after a colon at the end of a row or round denote(s) the number of stitches or spaces you should have on that row or round.

CROCHET HOOKS																	
U.S.	B-1	C-2	D-3	E-4	F-5	G-6	7	H-8	I-9	J-10	K-10½	L-11	M/N-13	N/P-15	P/Q	Q	S
Metric - mm	2.25	2.75	3.25	3.5	3.75	4	4.5	5	5.5	6	6.5	8	9	10	15	16	19

GAUGE

Exact gauge is **essential** for proper size. Before beginning your project, make the sample swatch given in the individual instructions in the yarn and hook specified. After completing the swatch, measure it, counting your stitches and rows carefully. If your swatch is larger or smaller than specified, **make another, changing hook size to get the correct gauge.** Keep trying until you find the size hook that will give you the specified gauge.

Yarn Weight Symbol & Names	LACE 0	SUPER FINE 1	FINE 2	LIGHT 3	MEDIUM 4	BULKY 5	SUPER BULKY 6
Type of Yarns in Category	Fingering, 10-count crochet thread	Sock, Fingering Baby	Sport, Baby	DK, Light Worsted	Worsted, Afghan, Aran	Chunky, Craft, Rug	Bulky, Roving
Crochet Gauge* Ranges in Single Crochet to 4" (10 cm)	32-42 double crochets**	21-32 sts	16-20 sts	12-17 sts	11-14 sts	8-11 sts	5-9 sts
Advised Hook Size Range	Steel*** 6,7,8 Regular hook B-1	B-1 to E-4	E-4 to 7	7 to I-9	I-9 to K-10½	K-10½ to M/N-13	M/N-13 and larger

*GUIDELINES ONLY: The chart above reflects the most commonly used gauges and hook sizes for specific yarn categories.

** Lace weight yarns are usually crocheted on larger-size hooks to create lacy openwork patterns. Accordingly, a gauge range is difficult to determine. Always follow the gauge stated in your pattern.

*** Steel crochet hooks are sized differently from regular hooks–the higher the number the smaller the hook, which is the reverse of regular hook sizing.

BEGINNER	Projects for first-time crocheters using basic stitches. Minimal shaping.
EASY	Projects using yarn with basic stitches, repetitive stitch patterns, simple color changes, and simple shaping and finishing.
INTERMEDIATE	Projects using a variety of techniques, such as basic lace patterns or color patterns, mid-level shaping and finishing.
EXPERIENCED	Projects with intricate stitch patterns, techniques and dimension, such as non-repeating patterns, multi-color techniques, fine threads, small hooks, detailed shaping and refined finishing.

BACK OR FRONT LOOPS ONLY

Work only in loop(s) indicated by arrow *(Fig. 1)*.

Fig. 1

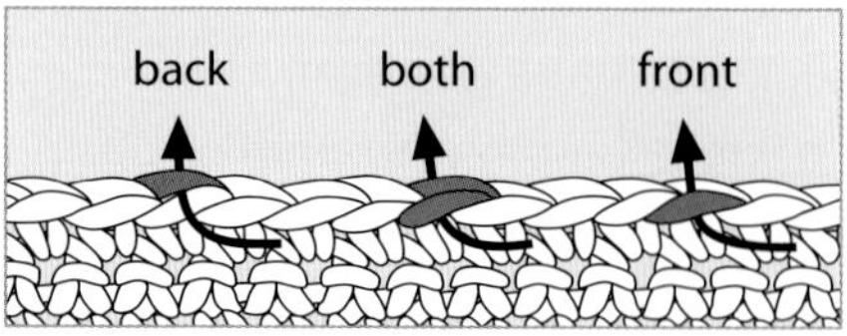

FREE LOOPS

After working in Back or Front Loops Only on a row, there will be a ridge of unused loops. These are called the free loops. Later, when instructed to work in the free loops of the same row, work in these loops *(Fig. 2a)*.

Fig. 2a

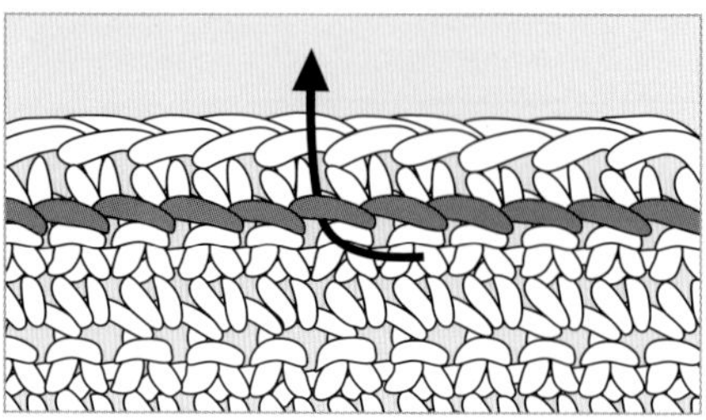

When instructed to work in free loops of a chain, work in loop indicated by arrow *(Fig. 2b)*.

Fig. 2b

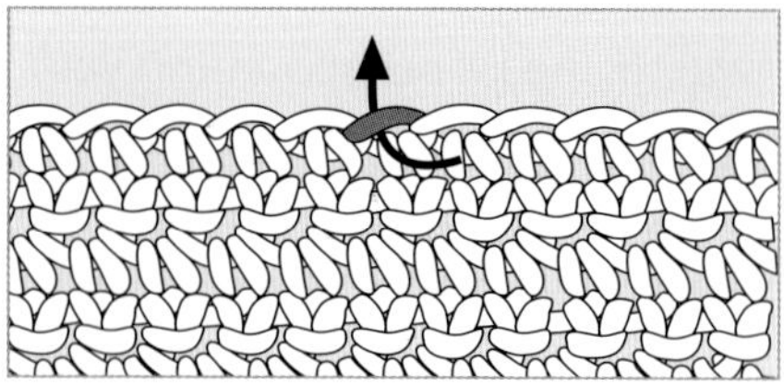

JOINING WITH SC

When instructed to join with sc, begin with a slip knot on hook. Insert hook in stitch or space indicated, YO and pull up a loop, (YO and draw through both loops on hook *(Fig. 3)*.

Fig. 3

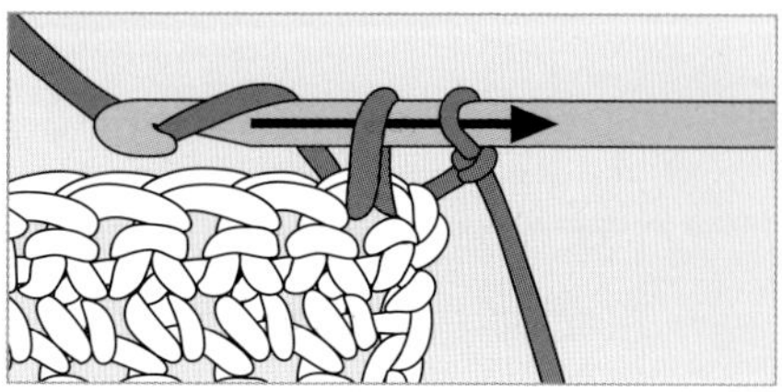

JOINING WITH DC

When instructed to join with dc, begin with a slip knot on hook. YO, holding loop on hook, insert hook in stitch or space indicated, YO and pull up a loop, (YO and draw through 2 loops on hook) twice *(Fig. 4)*.

Fig. 4

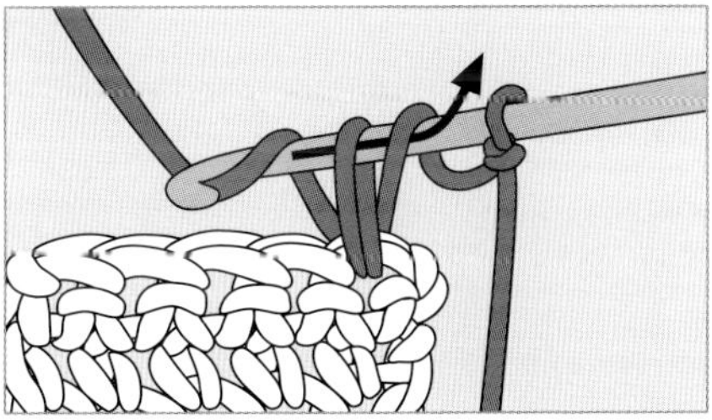

WHIPSTITCH

Place two Motifs, Strips, or edges with **wrong** sides together. Sew through both pieces once to secure the beginning of the seam, leaving an ample yarn end to weave in later. Insert the needle from **front** to **back** through **inside** loops only of each stitch on both pieces *(Fig. 5a)* **or** through **both** loops on both pieces *(Fig. 5b)* as specified. Bring the needle around and insert it from **front** to **back** through next loops of both pieces. Continue in this manner across, keeping the sewing yarn fairly loose.

Fig. 5a

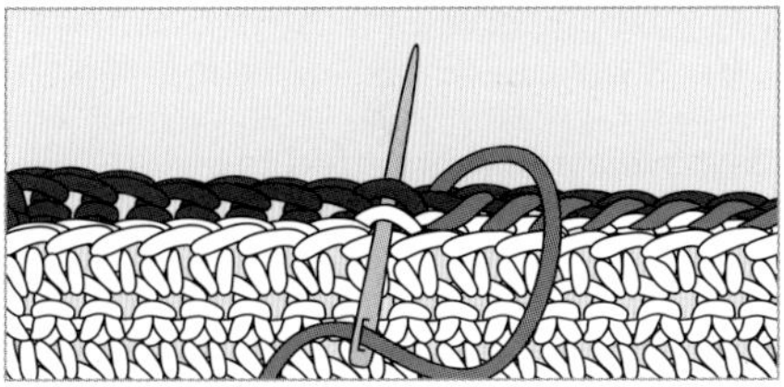

Fig. 5b

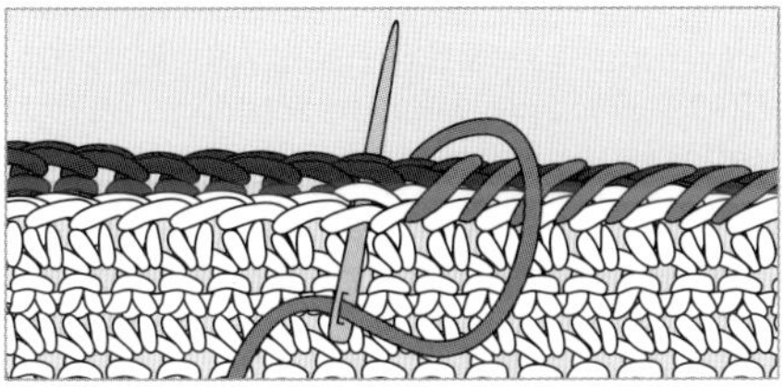

POM-POM

Cut a piece of cardboard 3" (7.5 cm) square.

Wind the yarn around the cardboard until it is approximately 1/2" (12 mm) thick in the middle *(Fig. 6a)*.

Carefully slip the yarn off the cardboard.

Fig. 6a

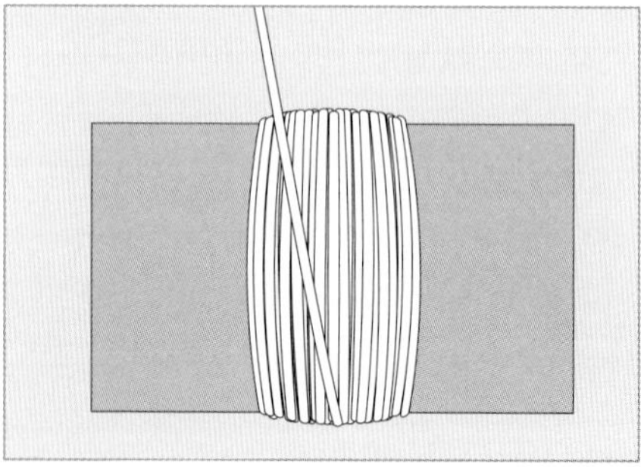

To add a pom-pom to the top of a hat, firmly tie an 18" (45.5 cm) length of yarn around the middle *(Fig. 6b)*. Leave yarn ends long enough to attach the pom-pom.

To add a pom-pom to the end of a tie, firmly tie the long yarn ends left on the tie around the middle *(Fig. 6b)*.

Cut the loops on both ends and trim the pom-pom into a smooth ball *(Fig. 6c)*.

Fig. 6b

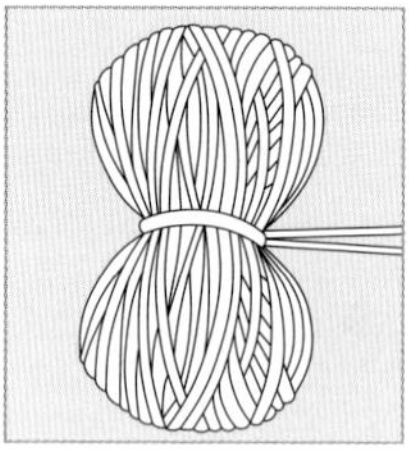

Fig. 6c

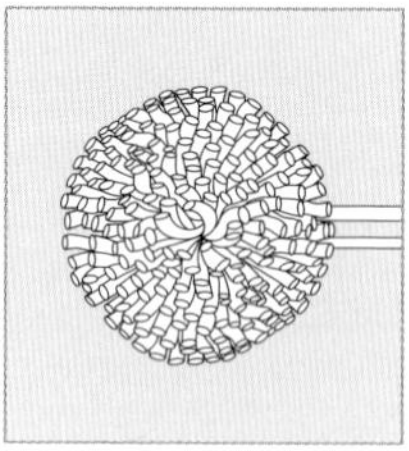

We have made every effort to ensure that these instructions are accurate and complete. We cannot, however, be responsible for human error, typographical mistakes, or variations in individual work.

Instructions tested and photo models made by Janet Akins and Marianna Crowder.

Production Team: Writer/Technical Editor - Cathy Hardy; Editorial Writer – Susan Frantz Wiles; Senior Graphic Artist – Lora Puls; Graphic Artist - Sharvil Salve; Photo Stylist - Sondra Daniel; and Photographer - Ken West.